THINGS MY

KID

SAID
TO
ME!

THIS JOURNAL BELONGS TO

_____

_____

DEDICATION

This Kids Quotes Journal log is dedicated to all the parents out there who want to record all the funny things their kids say and document their findings in the process.

You are my inspiration for producing books and I'm honored to be a part of keeping all of your child's quotes notes and records organized.

This journal notebook will help you record your details about your kid's hilarious and silly sayings.

Thoughtfully put together with these sections to record in detail: Date, Month, Today My Kid Said, How It Made Me Feel, Underlying Meaning, Did We Talk About It, & Notes.

HOW TO USE THIS BOOK

The purpose of this book is to keep all of your kids quotes and sayings notes all in one place. It will help keep you organized.

This Kid's Quotes Journal will allow you to accurately document every detail about the funny things your child says. It's a great way to chart your course through recording memories of their childhood.

Here are examples of the prompts for you to fill in and write about your experience in this book:

1. Date, Month

2. Today My Kid Said

3. How It Made Me Feel

4. Underlying meaning

5. Did We Talk About It

6. Notes

DATE: _____

MONTH: _____

TODAY MY KID

SAID TO ME!

_____

_____

_____

_____

HOW IT MADE ME FEEL

_____

_____

_____

_____

UNDERLYING MEANING?

_____

_____

*DID WE TALK ABOUT THIS
STATEMENT MADE?*

_____

_____

NOTES

_____

_____

DATE: _____

MONTH: _____

TODAY MY KID

SAID TO ME!

_____

_____

_____

_____

HOW IT MADE ME FEEL

_____

_____

_____

_____

UNDERLYING MEANING?

_____

_____

DID WE TALK ABOUT THIS STATEMENT MADE?

_____

_____

NOTES

_____

_____

DATE: _____
MONTH: _____

TODAY MY KID
SAID TO ME!

_____
_____
_____
_____

HOW IT MADE ME FEEL

_____
_____
_____
_____

UNDERLYING
MEANING?

_____
_____

DID WE TALK ABOUT THIS
STATEMENT MADE?

_____
_____

NOTES

_____
_____

DATE: _____
MONTH: _____

TODAY MY KID
SAID TO ME!

_____

_____

_____

_____

HOW IT MADE ME FEEL

_____

_____

_____

_____

UNDERLYING MEANING?

_____

_____

DID WE TALK ABOUT THIS STATEMENT MADE?

_____

_____

NOTES

_____

_____

DATE: _____

MONTH: _____

TODAY MY KID

SAID TO ME!

_____

_____

_____

_____

HOW IT MADE ME FEEL

_____

_____

_____

UNDERLYING MEANING?

_____

_____

DID WE TALK ABOUT THIS
STATEMENT MADE?

_____

_____

NOTES

_____

_____

DATE: _____

MONTH: _____

TODAY MY KID

SAID TO ME!

_____

_____

_____

_____

HOW IT MADE ME FEEL

_____

_____

_____

_____

UNDERLYING MEANING?

_____

_____

DID WE TALK ABOUT THIS STATEMENT MADE?

_____

_____

NOTES

_____

_____

DATE: _____

MONTH: _____

TODAY MY KID

SAID TO ME!

_____

_____

_____

_____

HOW IT MADE ME FEEL

_____

_____

_____

_____

UNDERLYING MEANING?

_____

_____

DID WE TALK ABOUT THIS STATEMENT MADE?

_____

_____

NOTES

_____

_____

DATE: _____

MONTH: _____

TODAY MY KID

SAID TO ME!

_____

_____

_____

_____

HOW IT MADE ME FEEL

_____

_____

_____

_____

UNDERLYING MEANING?

_____

_____

DID WE TALK ABOUT THIS STATEMENT MADE?

_____

_____

NOTES

_____

_____

DATE: _____
MONTH: _____

TODAY MY KID
SAID TO ME!

_____
_____
_____
_____

HOW IT MADE ME FEEL

_____
_____
_____
_____

UNDERLYING MEANING?

_____
_____

*DID WE TALK ABOUT THIS
STATEMENT MADE?*

_____
_____

NOTES

_____
_____

DATE: _____
MONTH: _____

TODAY MY KID
SAID TO ME!

_____

_____

_____

_____

HOW IT MADE ME FEEL

_____

_____

_____

UNDERLYING MEANING?

_____

_____

DID WE TALK ABOUT THIS STATEMENT MADE?

_____

_____

NOTES

_____

_____

DATE: _____

MONTH: _____

TODAY MY KID

SAID TO ME!

_____

_____

_____

_____

HOW IT MADE ME FEEL

_____

_____

_____

_____

UNDERLYING MEANING?

_____

_____

DID WE TALK ABOUT THIS STATEMENT MADE?

_____

_____

NOTES

_____

_____

DATE: _____

MONTH: _____

TODAY MY KID
SAID TO ME!

_____

_____

_____

_____

HOW IT MADE ME FEEL

_____

_____

_____

_____

UNDERLYING MEANING?

_____

_____

DID WE TALK ABOUT THIS
STATEMENT MADE?

_____

_____

NOTES

_____

_____

DATE: _____
MONTH: _____

TODAY MY KID
SAID TO ME!

_____
_____
_____
_____

HOW IT MADE ME FEEL

_____
_____
_____
_____

UNDERLYING
MEANING?

_____
_____

DID WE TALK ABOUT THIS
STATEMENT MADE?

_____
_____

NOTES

_____
_____

DATE: _____
MONTH: _____

TODAY MY KID
SAID TO ME!

_____
_____
_____
_____

HOW IT MADE ME FEEL

_____
_____
_____

UNDERLYING
MEANING?

_____
_____

*DID WE TALK ABOUT THIS
STATEMENT MADE?*

_____
_____

NOTES

_____
_____

DATE: _____

MONTH: _____

SAID TO ME!

_____

_____

_____

_____

HOW IT MADE ME FEEL

_____

_____

_____

_____

UNDERLYING MEANING?

_____

_____

*DID WE TALK ABOUT THIS
STATEMENT MADE?*

_____

_____

NOTES

_____

_____

DATE: _____
MONTH: _____

TODAY MY KID
SAID TO ME!

_____
_____
_____
_____

HOW IT MADE ME FEEL

_____
_____
_____

UNDERLYING MEANING?

_____
_____

*DID WE TALK ABOUT THIS
STATEMENT MADE?*

_____
_____

NOTES

_____
_____

DATE: _____
MONTH: _____

TODAY MY KID

SAID TO ME!

_____
_____
_____
_____

HOW IT MADE ME FEEL

_____
_____
_____
_____

UNDERLYING MEANING?

_____
_____

DID WE TALK ABOUT THIS
STATEMENT MADE?

_____
_____

NOTES

_____
_____

DATE: _____
MONTH: _____

TODAY MY KID
SAID TO ME!

_____
_____
_____
_____

HOW IT MADE ME FEEL

_____
_____
_____
_____

UNDERLYING MEANING?

_____
_____

DID WE TALK ABOUT THIS
STATEMENT MADE?

_____
_____

NOTES

_____
_____

DATE: _____

MONTH: _____

TODAY MY KID

SAID TO ME!

_____

_____

_____

_____

HOW IT MADE ME FEEL

_____

_____

_____

_____

UNDERLYING MEANING?

_____

_____

*DID WE TALK ABOUT THIS
STATEMENT MADE?*

_____

_____

NOTES

_____

_____

DATE: _____
MONTH: _____

TODAY MY KID
SAID TO ME!

_____
_____
_____
_____

HOW IT MADE ME FEEL

_____
_____
_____
_____

UNDERLYING MEANING?

_____
_____

DID WE TALK ABOUT THIS
STATEMENT MADE?

_____
_____

NOTES

_____
_____

DATE: _____

MONTH: _____

SAID TO ME!

_____

_____

_____

_____

HOW IT MADE ME FEEL

_____

_____

_____

_____

UNDERLYING
MEANING?

_____

_____

*DID WE TALK ABOUT THIS
STATEMENT MADE?*

_____

_____

NOTES

_____

_____

DATE: _____

MONTH: _____

TODAY MY KID

SAID TO ME!

_____

_____

_____

_____

HOW IT MADE ME FEEL

_____

_____

_____

_____

UNDERLYING MEANING?

_____

_____

DID WE TALK ABOUT THIS STATEMENT MADE?

_____

_____

NOTES

_____

_____

DATE: _____

MONTH: _____

TODAY MY KID
SAID TO ME!

_____
_____
_____
_____

HOW IT MADE ME FEEL

_____
_____
_____
_____

UNDERLYING
MEANING?

_____
_____

DID WE TALK ABOUT THIS
STATEMENT MADE?

_____
_____

NOTES

_____
_____

DATE: _____

MONTH: _____

TODAY MY KID
SAID TO ME!

_____

_____

_____

_____

HOW IT MADE ME FEEL

_____

_____

_____

UNDERLYING MEANING?

_____

_____

DID WE TALK ABOUT THIS STATEMENT MADE?

_____

_____

NOTES

_____

_____

DATE: _____

MONTH: _____

TODAY MY KID
SAID TO ME!

_____

_____

_____

_____

HOW IT MADE ME FEEL

_____

_____

_____

_____

UNDERLYING MEANING?

_____

_____

DID WE TALK ABOUT THIS
STATEMENT MADE?

_____

_____

NOTES

_____

_____

DATE: _____
MONTH: _____

SAID TO ME!

_____
_____
_____
_____

HOW IT MADE ME FEEL

_____
_____
_____
_____

UNDERLYING MEANING?

_____
_____

DID WE TALK ABOUT THIS STATEMENT MADE?

_____
_____

NOTES

_____
_____

DATE: _____
MONTH: _____

TODAY MY KID
SAID TO ME!

_____

_____

_____

_____

HOW IT MADE ME FEEL

_____

_____

_____

_____

UNDERLYING
MEANING?

_____

_____

DID WE TALK ABOUT THIS
STATEMENT MADE?

_____

_____

NOTES

_____

_____

DATE: _____
MONTH: _____

TODAY MY KID
SAID TO ME!

_____
_____
_____
_____

HOW IT MADE ME FEEL

_____
_____
_____
_____

UNDERLYING MEANING?

_____
_____

DID WE TALK ABOUT THIS
STATEMENT MADE?

_____
_____

NOTES

_____
_____

DATE: _____
MONTH: _____

TODAY MY KID
SAID TO ME!

_____
_____
_____
_____

HOW IT MADE ME FEEL

_____
_____
_____
_____

UNDERLYING MEANING?

_____
_____

DID WE TALK ABOUT THIS
STATEMENT MADE?

_____
_____

NOTES

_____
_____

DATE: _____
MONTH: _____

TODAY MY KID
SAID TO ME!

_____
_____
_____
_____

HOW IT MADE ME FEEL

_____
_____
_____
_____

UNDERLYING MEANING?

_____
_____

DID WE TALK ABOUT THIS
STATEMENT MADE?

_____
_____

NOTES

_____
_____

DATE: _____

MONTH: _____

TODAY MY KID

SAID TO ME!

_____

_____

_____

_____

HOW IT MADE ME FEEL

_____

_____

_____

_____

UNDERLYING MEANING?

_____

_____

DID WE TALK ABOUT THIS STATEMENT MADE?

_____

_____

NOTES

_____

_____

DATE: _____
MONTH: _____

TODAY MY KID
SAID TO ME!

_____
_____
_____
_____

HOW IT MADE ME FEEL

_____
_____
_____

UNDERLYING MEANING?

_____
_____

DID WE TALK ABOUT THIS STATEMENT MADE?

_____
_____

NOTES

_____
_____

DATE: _____
MONTH: _____

TODAY MY KID
SAID TO ME!

_____
_____
_____
_____

HOW IT MADE ME FEEL

_____
_____
_____

UNDERLYING MEANING?

_____
_____

DID WE TALK ABOUT THIS
STATEMENT MADE?

_____
_____

NOTES

_____
_____

DATE: ————————————————

MONTH: ————————————————

TODAY MY KID

SAID TO ME!

————————————————

————————————————

————————————————

————————————————

HOW IT MADE ME FEEL

————————————————

————————————————

————————————————

————————————————

UNDERLYING MEANING?

————————————————

————————————————

DID WE TALK ABOUT THIS
STATEMENT MADE?

————————————————

————————————————

NOTES

————————————————

————————————————

DATE: _____

MONTH: _____

TODAY MY KID
SAID TO ME!

_____

_____

_____

_____

HOW IT MADE ME FEEL

_____

_____

_____

_____

UNDERLYING
MEANING?

_____

_____

*DID WE TALK ABOUT THIS
STATEMENT MADE?*

_____

_____

NOTES

_____

_____

DATE: _____

MONTH: _____

SAID TO ME!

_____

_____

_____

_____

HOW IT MADE ME FEEL

_____

_____

_____

UNDERLYING MEANING?

_____

_____

DID WE TALK ABOUT THIS STATEMENT MADE?

_____

_____

NOTES

_____

_____

DATE: _____

MONTH: _____

SAID TO ME!

_____

_____

_____

_____

HOW IT MADE ME FEEL

_____

_____

_____

_____

UNDERLYING MEANING?

_____

_____

DID WE TALK ABOUT THIS STATEMENT MADE?

_____

_____

NOTES

_____

_____

DATE: _____

MONTH: _____

TODAY MY KID
SAID TO ME!

_____

_____

_____

_____

HOW IT MADE ME FEEL

_____

_____

_____

UNDERLYING MEANING?

_____

_____

*DID WE TALK ABOUT THIS
STATEMENT MADE?*

_____

_____

NOTES

_____

_____

DATE: ———————————————

MONTH: ———————————————

TODAY MY KID

SAID TO ME!

———————————————

———————————————

———————————————

———————————————

HOW IT MADE ME FEEL

———————————————

———————————————

———————————————

———————————————

UNDERLYING MEANING?

———————————————

———————————————

DID WE TALK ABOUT THIS
STATEMENT MADE?

———————————————

———————————————

NOTES

———————————————

———————————————

DATE: _____
MONTH: _____

TODAY MY KID
SAID TO ME!

_____
_____
_____
_____

HOW IT MADE ME FEEL

_____
_____
_____
_____

UNDERLYING
MEANING?

_____
_____

DID WE TALK ABOUT THIS
STATEMENT MADE?

_____
_____

NOTES

_____
_____

DATE: _____

MONTH: _____

TODAY MY KID
SAID TO ME!

_____

_____

_____

_____

HOW IT MADE ME FEEL

_____

_____

_____

_____

UNDERLYING
MEANING?

_____

_____

DID WE TALK ABOUT THIS
STATEMENT MADE?

_____

_____

NOTES

_____

_____

DATE: _____
MONTH: _____

TODAY MY KID
SAID TO ME!

_____

_____

_____

_____

HOW IT MADE ME FEEL

_____

_____

_____

UNDERLYING MEANING?

_____

_____

DID WE TALK ABOUT THIS STATEMENT MADE?

_____

_____

NOTES

_____

_____

DATE: _____

MONTH: _____

TODAY MY KID
SAID TO ME!

_____

_____

_____

_____

HOW IT MADE ME FEEL

_____

_____

_____

_____

UNDERLYING
MEANING?

_____

_____

DID WE TALK ABOUT THIS
STATEMENT MADE?

_____

_____

NOTES

_____

_____

DATE: _____
MONTH: _____

TODAY MY KID
SAID TO ME!

_____
_____
_____
_____

HOW IT MADE ME FEEL

_____
_____
_____
_____

UNDERLYING MEANING?

_____
_____

*DID WE TALK ABOUT THIS
STATEMENT MADE?*

_____
_____

NOTES

_____
_____

DATE: _____

MONTH: _____

TODAY MY KID

SAID TO ME!

_____

_____

_____

_____

HOW IT MADE ME FEEL

_____

_____

_____

_____

UNDERLYING MEANING?

_____

_____

*DID WE TALK ABOUT THIS
STATEMENT MADE?*

_____

_____

NOTES

_____

_____

DATE: _____
MONTH: _____

TODAY MY KID
SAID TO ME!

_____
_____
_____
_____

HOW IT MADE ME FEEL

_____
_____
_____
_____

UNDERLYING MEANING?

_____
_____

DID WE TALK ABOUT THIS
STATEMENT MADE?

_____
_____

NOTES

_____
_____

DATE: _____
MONTH: _____

TODAY MY KID
SAID TO ME!

_____
_____
_____
_____

HOW IT MADE ME FEEL

_____
_____
_____
_____

UNDERLYING MEANING?

_____
_____

DID WE TALK ABOUT THIS
STATEMENT MADE?

_____
_____

NOTES

_____
_____

DATE: _____
MONTH: _____

TODAY MY KID
SAID TO ME!

_____
_____
_____
_____

HOW IT MADE ME FEEL

_____
_____
_____
_____

UNDERLYING
MEANING?

_____
_____

DID WE TALK ABOUT THIS
STATEMENT MADE?

_____
_____

NOTES

_____
_____

DATE: _____

MONTH: _____

TODAY MY KID
SAID TO ME!

_____
_____
_____
_____

HOW IT MADE ME FEEL

_____
_____
_____
_____

UNDERLYING
MEANING?

_____
_____

DID WE TALK ABOUT THIS
STATEMENT MADE?

_____
_____

NOTES

_____
_____

DATE: _____

MONTH: _____

TODAY MY KID

SAID TO ME!

_____

_____

_____

HOW IT MADE ME FEEL

_____

_____

_____

UNDERLYING MEANING?

_____

_____

DID WE TALK ABOUT THIS STATEMENT MADE?

_____

_____

NOTES

_____

_____

DATE: _____

MONTH: _____

TODAY MY KID
SAID TO ME!

_____

_____

_____

_____

HOW IT MADE ME FEEL

_____

_____

_____

UNDERLYING
MEANING?

_____

_____

DID WE TALK ABOUT THIS
STATEMENT MADE?

_____

_____

NOTES

_____

_____

DATE: _____

MONTH: _____

TODAY MY KID
SAID TO ME!

_____

_____

_____

_____

HOW IT MADE ME FEEL

_____

_____

_____

_____

UNDERLYING
MEANING?

_____

_____

DID WE TALK ABOUT THIS
STATEMENT MADE?

_____

_____

NOTES

_____

_____

DATE: _____
MONTH: _____

_____
_____
_____
_____

HOW IT MADE ME FEEL

_____
_____
_____
_____

UNDERLYING MEANING?

_____
_____

DID WE TALK ABOUT THIS
STATEMENT MADE?

_____
_____

NOTES

_____
_____

DATE: _____

MONTH: _____

TODAY MY KID
SAID TO ME!

_____

_____

_____

_____

HOW IT MADE ME FEEL

_____

_____

_____

_____

UNDERLYING MEANING?

_____

_____

DID WE TALK ABOUT THIS STATEMENT MADE?

_____

_____

NOTES

_____

_____

DATE: _____

MONTH: _____

SAID TO ME!

_____

_____

_____

_____

HOW IT MADE ME FEEL

_____

_____

_____

_____

UNDERLYING MEANING?

_____

_____

*DID WE TALK ABOUT THIS
STATEMENT MADE?*

_____

_____

NOTES

_____

_____

DATE: _____
MONTH: _____

TODAY MY KID
SAID TO ME!

_____

_____

_____

_____

HOW IT MADE ME FEEL

_____

_____

_____

_____

UNDERLYING
MEANING?

_____

_____

DID WE TALK ABOUT THIS
STATEMENT MADE?

_____

_____

NOTES

_____

_____

DATE: _____
MONTH: _____

TODAY MY KID
SAID TO ME!

_____

_____

_____

_____

HOW IT MADE ME FEEL

_____

_____

_____

UNDERLYING
MEANING?

_____

_____

*DID WE TALK ABOUT THIS
STATEMENT MADE?*

_____

_____

NOTES

_____

_____

DATE: _____
MONTH: _____

TODAY MY KID
SAID TO ME!

_____
_____
_____
_____

HOW IT MADE ME FEEL

_____
_____
_____

UNDERLYING MEANING?

_____
_____

DID WE TALK ABOUT THIS
STATEMENT MADE?

_____
_____

NOTES

_____
_____

DATE: _____

MONTH: _____

TODAY MY KID

SAID TO ME!

_____

_____

_____

_____

HOW IT MADE ME FEEL

_____

_____

_____

_____

UNDERLYING MEANING?

_____

_____

DID WE TALK ABOUT THIS STATEMENT MADE?

_____

_____

NOTES

_____

_____

DATE: _____

MONTH: _____

TODAY MY KID
SAID TO ME!

_____

_____

_____

_____

HOW IT MADE ME FEEL

_____

_____

_____

UNDERLYING MEANING?

_____

_____

DID WE TALK ABOUT THIS STATEMENT MADE?

_____

_____

NOTES

_____

_____

DATE: _____

MONTH: _____

SAID TO ME!

_____

_____

_____

_____

HOW IT MADE ME FEEL

_____

_____

_____

UNDERLYING MEANING?

_____

_____

DID WE TALK ABOUT THIS STATEMENT MADE?

_____

_____

NOTES

_____

_____

DATE: _____

MONTH: _____

TODAY MY KID
SAID TO ME!

_____
_____
_____
_____

HOW IT MADE ME FEEL

_____
_____
_____
_____

UNDERLYING
MEANING?

_____
_____

*DID WE TALK ABOUT THIS
STATEMENT MADE?*

_____
_____

NOTES

_____
_____

DATE: _____

MONTH: _____

TODAY MY KID

SAID TO ME!

_____

_____

_____

_____

HOW IT MADE ME FEEL

_____

_____

_____

_____

UNDERLYING MEANING?

_____

_____

DID WE TALK ABOUT THIS STATEMENT MADE?

_____

_____

NOTES

_____

_____

DATE: _____
MONTH: _____

SAID TO ME!

_____
_____
_____
_____

HOW IT MADE ME FEEL

_____
_____
_____
_____

UNDERLYING MEANING?

_____
_____

DID WE TALK ABOUT THIS STATEMENT MADE?

_____
_____

NOTES

_____
_____

DATE: _____
MONTH: _____

TODAY MY KID
SAID TO ME!

_____
_____
_____
_____

HOW IT MADE ME FEEL

_____
_____
_____
_____

UNDERLYING MEANING?

_____
_____

DID WE TALK ABOUT THIS
STATEMENT MADE?

_____
_____

NOTES

_____
_____

DATE: _____
MONTH: _____

TODAY MY KID
SAID TO ME!

_____
_____
_____
_____

HOW IT MADE ME FEEL

_____
_____
_____
_____

UNDERLYING MEANING?

_____
_____

DID WE TALK ABOUT THIS
STATEMENT MADE?

_____
_____

NOTES

_____
_____

DATE: _____
MONTH: _____

SAID TO ME!

_____
_____
_____
_____

HOW IT MADE ME FEEL

_____
_____
_____
_____

UNDERLYING MEANING?

_____
_____

DID WE TALK ABOUT THIS STATEMENT MADE?

_____
_____

NOTES

_____
_____

DATE: _____

MONTH: _____

SAID TO ME!

_____

_____

_____

_____

HOW IT MADE ME FEEL

_____

_____

_____

_____

UNDERLYING MEANING?

_____

_____

*DID WE TALK ABOUT THIS
STATEMENT MADE?*

_____

_____

NOTES

_____

_____

DATE: _____
MONTH: _____

TODAY MY KID
SAID TO ME!

_____
_____
_____
_____

HOW IT MADE ME FEEL

_____
_____
_____
_____

UNDERLYING
MEANING?

_____
_____

DID WE TALK ABOUT THIS
STATEMENT MADE?

_____
_____

NOTES

_____
_____

DATE: _____

MONTH: _____

SAID TO ME!

_____

_____

_____

_____

HOW IT MADE ME FEEL

_____

_____

_____

_____

UNDERLYING MEANING?

_____

_____

DID WE TALK ABOUT THIS STATEMENT MADE?

_____

_____

NOTES

_____

_____

DATE: _____

MONTH: _____

TODAY MY KID

SAID TO ME!

_____

_____

_____

_____

HOW IT MADE ME FEEL

_____

_____

_____

_____

UNDERLYING MEANING?

_____

_____

DID WE TALK ABOUT THIS STATEMENT MADE?

_____

_____

NOTES

_____

_____

DATE: _____
MONTH: _____

TODAY MY KID
SAID TO ME!

_____
_____
_____
_____

HOW IT MADE ME FEEL

_____
_____
_____
_____

UNDERLYING MEANING?

_____
_____

DID WE TALK ABOUT THIS
STATEMENT MADE?

_____
_____

NOTES

_____
_____

DATE: _____
MONTH: _____

TODAY MY KID
SAID TO ME!

_____
_____
_____
_____

HOW IT MADE ME FEEL

_____
_____
_____

UNDERLYING
MEANING?

_____
_____

DID WE TALK ABOUT THIS
STATEMENT MADE?

_____
_____

NOTES

_____
_____

DATE: _____
MONTH: _____

TODAY MY KID
SAID TO ME!

_____
_____
_____
_____

HOW IT MADE ME FEEL

_____
_____
_____
_____

UNDERLYING MEANING?

_____
_____

DID WE TALK ABOUT THIS
STATEMENT MADE?

_____
_____

NOTES

_____
_____

DATE: _____
MONTH: _____

TODAY MY KID
SAID TO ME!

_____
_____
_____
_____

HOW IT MADE ME FEEL

_____
_____
_____
_____

UNDERLYING
MEANING?

_____
_____

DID WE TALK ABOUT THIS
STATEMENT MADE?

_____
_____

NOTES

_____
_____

DATE: _____
MONTH: _____

SAID TO ME!

_____
_____
_____
_____

HOW IT MADE ME FEEL

_____
_____
_____
_____

UNDERLYING MEANING?

_____
_____

*DID WE TALK ABOUT THIS
STATEMENT MADE?*

_____
_____

NOTES

_____
_____

DATE: _____

MONTH: _____

SAID TO ME!

_____

_____

_____

_____

HOW IT MADE ME FEEL

_____

_____

_____

_____

UNDERLYING MEANING?

_____

_____

DID WE TALK ABOUT THIS STATEMENT MADE?

_____

_____

NOTES

_____

_____

DATE: _____
MONTH: _____

TODAY MY KID
SAID TO ME!

_____
_____
_____
_____

HOW IT MADE ME FEEL

_____
_____
_____
_____

UNDERLYING MEANING?

_____
_____

*DID WE TALK ABOUT THIS
STATEMENT MADE?*

_____
_____

NOTES

_____
_____

DATE: _____

MONTH: _____

TODAY MY KID

SAID TO ME!

_____

_____

_____

_____

HOW IT MADE ME FEEL

_____

_____

_____

_____

UNDERLYING MEANING?

_____

_____

*DID WE TALK ABOUT THIS
STATEMENT MADE?*

_____

_____

NOTES

_____

_____

DATE: _____

MONTH: _____

SAID TO ME!

_____

_____

_____

_____

HOW IT MADE ME FEEL

_____

_____

_____

_____

UNDERLYING MEANING?

_____

_____

DID WE TALK ABOUT THIS STATEMENT MADE?

_____

_____

NOTES

_____

_____

DATE: _____
MONTH: _____

TODAY MY KID
SAID TO ME!

_____
_____
_____
_____

HOW IT MADE ME FEEL

_____
_____
_____
_____

UNDERLYING
MEANING?

_____
_____

*DID WE TALK ABOUT THIS
STATEMENT MADE?*

_____
_____

NOTES

_____
_____

DATE: _____
MONTH: _____

TODAY MY KID
SAID TO ME!

_____
_____
_____
_____

HOW IT MADE ME FEEL

_____
_____
_____
_____

UNDERLYING MEANING?

_____
_____

DID WE TALK ABOUT THIS STATEMENT MADE?

_____
_____

NOTES

_____
_____

DATE: _____
MONTH: _____

TODAY MY KID
SAID TO ME!

_____
_____
_____
_____

HOW IT MADE ME FEEL

_____
_____
_____

UNDERLYING
MEANING?

_____
_____

DID WE TALK ABOUT THIS
STATEMENT MADE?

_____
_____

NOTES

_____
_____

DATE: _____
MONTH: _____

TODAY MY KID
SAID TO ME!

_____
_____
_____

HOW IT MADE ME FEEL

_____
_____
_____

UNDERLYING
MEANING?

_____
_____

DID WE TALK ABOUT THIS
STATEMENT MADE?

_____
_____

NOTES

_____
_____

DATE: _____

MONTH: _____

TODAY MY KID
SAID TO ME!

_____
_____
_____
_____

HOW IT MADE ME FEEL

_____
_____
_____

UNDERLYING MEANING?

_____
_____

DID WE TALK ABOUT THIS STATEMENT MADE?

_____
_____

NOTES

_____
_____

DATE: _____

MONTH: _____

TODAY MY KID
SAID TO ME!

_____

_____

_____

_____

HOW IT MADE ME FEEL

_____

_____

_____

_____

UNDERLYING MEANING?

_____

_____

DID WE TALK ABOUT THIS STATEMENT MADE?

_____

_____

NOTES

_____

_____

DATE: _____
MONTH: _____

TODAY MY KID
SAID TO ME!

_____
_____
_____
_____

HOW IT MADE ME FEEL

_____
_____
_____
_____

UNDERLYING
MEANING?

_____
_____

DID WE TALK ABOUT THIS
STATEMENT MADE?

_____
_____

NOTES

_____
_____

DATE: _____
MONTH: _____

TODAY MY KID
SAID TO ME!

_____
_____
_____
_____

HOW IT MADE ME FEEL

_____
_____
_____
_____

UNDERLYING
MEANING?

_____
_____

DID WE TALK ABOUT THIS
STATEMENT MADE?

_____
_____

NOTES

_____
_____

DATE: _____
MONTH: _____

TODAY MY KID
SAID TO ME!

_____
_____
_____
_____

HOW IT MADE ME FEEL

_____
_____
_____

UNDERLYING
MEANING?

_____
_____

DID WE TALK ABOUT THIS
STATEMENT MADE?

_____
_____

NOTES

_____
_____

DATE: _____

MONTH: _____

TODAY MY KID
SAID TO ME!

_____

_____

_____

_____

HOW IT MADE ME FEEL

_____

_____

_____

_____

UNDERLYING
MEANING?

_____

_____

DID WE TALK ABOUT THIS
STATEMENT MADE?

_____

_____

NOTES

_____

_____

www.ingramcontent.com/pod-product-compliance
Lightning Source LLC
Chambersburg PA
CBHW051035030426
42336CB00015B/2882